God
Helpers

E.C. Russell

DEDICATION

To all the people who are feeling helpless or have felt helpless at one time or another, I dedicate this book to you.

CONTENTS

INTRODUCTION

We live in desperate, troubled times when millions are seeking help. I'm a baby boomer who grew up in Memphis, Tennessee—the home of Elvis Presley, the blues, and great Bar-b-q. The mighty Mississippi River flows with great majesty on the west side of Memphis that captivates the hearts of locals and tourists year after year. Memphis was a beautiful place to grow up, but it had its share of problems. On April 4, 1968, a year after I graduated from high school, Martin Luther King Jr. was assassinated at the Lorraine Motel. I remember vividly the riots that broke out following his death. Five years later, the federal government ordered desegregated busing in Memphis. As a result, massive fights broke out in the public schools.

Let's face it—we all need help. Whether you are stranded on the side of the road with a flat tire, juggling toddlers at home, or are faced with the devastation of losing a loved one, we all need support to maintain our well-being, achieve our goals, and live our fullest life. The help we need may be in the form of financial assistance, physical healing, marriage reconciliation, mental health services, companionship, education, sports, or just answers to life. It's hard to go through life without asking for some kind of help. Sometimes we look to our family, friends, coworkers, the government, God, or the church for help. This book is about discovering the help

God has for you and the avenues through which
He will deliver it.
Having drawn on many sources of support in my
life—including incredible friends and family—I
can say my greatest help has come from Jesus.
My best day was when I accepted Jesus as my
Lord. Before that day, I struggled with drinking.
This behavior brought a lot of pain and confusion
into my marriage with my wife Brenda. God,
through His great grace, helped me stop
drinking and heal my marriage.

God's heart and desire to help mankind can
be seen as early as creation. God knew man could
not thrive alone and that he would need help, so
he created woman (Genesis 2:18). Since then,
man and woman have been a natural help to one
another. This book will help you discover other
areas of natural help God provides for us.

Not only does God use people around us,
but he also provides supernatural help which
supersedes anything people can do. There is no
parallel to God's shear power. He helped the
prophet Elijah with an army of angels at the city
of Dothan in 2 Kings 6. He provided help in a
way our natural eyes could not see, because we
may not have our eyes open to things of God, to
the unseen help He is providing. This book will
help you recognize and receive this supernatural
help.

The original 12 disciples who followed Jesus

were men from all walks of life. Some were fishermen, one was a tax collector, one was a religious fanatic, and one was even a thief. The disciples of Jesus were fearful at the thought of Him leaving them to return to Heaven. He had fed them, protected them from storms, and they had seen Jesus perform countless miracles. Jesus made it clear to His disciples He would not leave them without help (John 14:15-18, John 16:7). That help came in the form of the Holy Spirit— our God-given helper, which I write about in the first section of this book along with God's word.

In the second section, I write about angels, faith, and the name of Jesus. In the third section, you will read about the blood of Jesus and people. Sometimes these helps may work together or separately, but they are God-given.

God not only cares for you, He is reaching out today through the Holy Spirit to help you. This book was written to show you some of the various ways God instructs and inspires you to receive help. At the end of each chapter you will find brief study questions which will help you in your search for help and to become more aware of God's plan for you. I pray as you read through these chapters you will find that God is not only a God who constantly reaches out to help you, but He is a God of love.

Remember, help is always closer than you think.

1
THE HOLY SPIRIT

The call for help can come at the most unexpected places and times. It was Sunday night, February 17, 2002. After our revival service, I was eating at McDonalds with the Rev. Herbert Cooper, my wife, and several families from First Assembly of God, which was the church I pastored. Rev. Cooper was our guest evangelist for that week. While we were eating, I noticed a Jackson police officer in the parking lot with his blue lights flashing. He was motioning for me to come outside. I immediately complied, only to be met with the tragic news that Alabama State Trooper Brian Nichols had been killed. His patrol vehicle hit a horse that was standing in the road. Needless to say, I was devastated. I was Brian's pastor for eight years, and because I served as a police chaplain, we had worked closely together on the police force. Just the night before, he and I had worked drivers' license checkpoints. Not only was Brian a leader in my church, he was a dear friend.

Devastated that I had lost my friend, I quickly pulled myself together to complete my next duty-- tell his wife and two children that he had been killed in a car accident. Somehow, I had to try to bring comfort to them, but I was struggling to work through my own shock and grief. I knew the only way to help his family would be by the Holy Spirit.

Brian's wife, children, and in-laws saw the trooper's car pull up and met us in the front yard. I told them Brian had passed. All I could hear were the cries of his family. All I could see were the looks of devastation in their eyes. We went into the house. Minutes later, Brian's captain, numerous Alabama State Troopers, other law enforcement officers, family, and friends gathered to talk and pray. The prayers and outpouring of love by so many brought a sense of God's presence to the grieving and broken-hearted. Later that night Brian's wife, Denise, came to the sad realization that funeral arrangements had to be made. Knowing Brian was a devoted Christian and God was guiding her with His presence made what seemed to be an impossible task possible.

There were more than 2,000 people in attendance at the visitation service at the First

Assembly of God. It took several hours for the last guests to pay their final respects to Brian. Even though the sorrow and grief seemed unbearable that night, God's presence was evident. The next day, more than 1,200 people attended the funeral service. The family and I prayed earnestly for God's guidance. Law enforcement officers from various agencies across the nation attended the funeral. Governor Don Siegelman was also there and met with the family prior to the service. People who had only met Brian on a few occasions came. The crowd was so large that we had to setup an overflow room in our Family Life Center to view the service through a projector. Despite the tragic circumstances, God met us! After I had preached, I gave an invitation and 37 people who were hurting and needing forgiveness of sins stood and prayed to receive Christ as their savior, one of whom was Governor Don Siegelman.

It was a long and painful road for Brian's loved ones, but God—by the Holy Spirit—helped them by His continued presence. He reassured them Brian was in heaven and walked each day with Brian's family and friends.

You may be experiencing something traumatic in your life at this very moment. God wants to help you by the person of the Holy Spirit. This help comes by His presence, even during the most difficult times. The Bible teaches that the Holy Spirit is a divine person and has always existed. The Holy Spirit was present at the creation of the world (Genesis 1:2). He is seen throughout the Old and New Testaments and is the "third person" of the Trinity. While the terms "third person" and "Trinity" are not found in the scriptures, they do help us to get a better understanding of the Godhead. The Divine Trinity is made up of three separate and distinct persons which are called God the Father, God the Son, and God the Holy Spirit. No person in the Godhead exists or works independently of the other (John 5:17-30). Concerning salvation, the Father planned it, the Son purchased it, and the Holy Spirit provides it (Eph. 1:3-14).

The scriptures teach that the Holy Spirit has characteristics just like God and Jesus. The Holy Spirit is called God (Acts 5:3-4), is omnipresent (Psalm 139:7-10), is omniscient (1 Corinthians 2:10-11), and is eternal (Hebrews 9:14). The Holy Spirit is also a living person that has emotions, intellect, and will. Jesus never referred to the Holy Spirit as "it" but as 'He." Jesus called the Holy Spirit "helper" (John 14:16). The helper— the Holy Spirit— teaches us, guides us, speaks to us, imparts love, gives power, invites men to Christ, helps us to pray, and gives us access to God.

Jesus was conceived by the Holy Spirit (Luke 1:35), Jesus was led by the Holy Spirit (Matthew 4:1), Jesus healed the sick by the Holy

Spirit (Acts 10:38), and He was raised from the dead by the Holy Spirit (Romans 8:11). The Holy Spirit helped Jesus in every aspect of His life and ministry. If the Holy Spirit helped Jesus, who was perfect, how much more enthusiastically should we seek the Holy Spirit to help us?

Encountering the Holy Spirit

The first encounter we have with the Holy Spirit is when He convicts us or shows us the sin of not believing in Jesus (John 16:8). The one and only sin the Holy Spirit will convict a non-believer of is the sin of not believing in Jesus. When that happens, we can either turn to the Lord or reject Him. Does the Holy Spirit convict us of sin once we're Christians? Yes, He does. It was on a Sunday morning in August 1975 at Fundamental Bible Church in Memphis when I received Jesus into my heart. My mother-in-law had invited me to her church several times before I finally went with her. I had been in and out of church for a long time, and I even remembered giving my heart to Jesus as a nine-year-old boy. However, something was different about this Sunday morning in Memphis; the Holy Spirit began to touch and convict me of the sin of not believing in Jesus. The Holy Spirit draws us to God. I knew I was away from God, and my heart was not right. We do not have to make deals with the Lord, but I still said, "Lord, if you will help me, I will live and serve you the rest of my life!" I desperately needed to bring my life and family back to a relationship with the Lord. I realized the need to be set free from sinful habits and to live a life of serving the Lord. My life was changed forever on that day.

The services at Fundamental Bible Church were completely different from any church I had attended before. People were excited. They did not attend the service passively. They did not treat church like another mundane obligation such as mowing the grass or grocery shopping. That was not the case at all! People were engaged, and God's presence was evident everywhere. People were lifting their hands, dancing, running up and down the aisles of the church, and even speaking in tongues. At first, it scared me, but after a while I realized the people were filled with the power and presence of the Holy Spirit. I had never attended a Pentecostal church before, so it was a completely new experience for me. That day I received Jesus into my heart, but I also realized what these church members had was from God. As I learned more about the Bible, I realized there was a deeper life in the Holy Spirit. If we receive Jesus, we receive the Holy Spirit in equal measure (Gal. 4:6).

The Holy Spirit Guides (John 16:13)

After we place our faith in Jesus, the Holy Spirit is present to guide us (John 16:13). Everyone needs guidance. Have you ever heard the statement, "let your conscience be your guide?" The only problem with letting our conscience guide us is that our conscience is governed by our own standard of conduct. We can be stuck in our own fears and unbelief—our lack and unworthiness—that are lies of the natural, physical world, not a spiritual truth. The Bible teaches that there are several types of conscience: good conscience (Hebrews 13:18), weak conscience (1 Corinthians 8:12), evil conscience (Hebrews 10:22), defiled conscience (Titus 1:15), seared conscience (1 Timothy 4:2), and pure conscience (2 Timothy 1:3).

However, we cannot let our conscience guide us unless the Holy Spirit guides our conscience. The Holy Spirit provides a consistency and integrity that our conscience does not. Jesus was guided by the Holy Spirit (Matthew 4:1), the Apostle Paul was guided by the Holy Spirit (Acts 13:2), and Christians are guided by the Holy Spirit (Romans 8:14). Purpose in your heart to let the Holy Spirit guide you. We need guidance for our families, our job opportunities, our marriages, our service to God, and in the day-to-day decisions we have to make.

Being Filled with the Holy Spirit

God had begun working in my life, and I desired to have more of Him, but I wasn't sure how that could happen. The answer was to be filled with the Holy Spirit. I know there were some things I couldn't overcome without the help of the Holy Spirit, so I began to seek God and ask him to fill me with the Holy Spirit. One afternoon I listened to some tapes by an evangelist; one was called "Modern Day Arguments Against the Holy Spirit," and the other was "How to Be Filled With the Holy Spirit." The teachings and messages on those tapes answered a lot of questions for me.

Later that night, my mother-in-law and I went to a revival service where a Baptist preacher was speaking. He had been filled with the Holy Spirit and spoke in tongues. After he was through preaching, he gave an altar call for those who needed to be saved, healed, or filled with the Holy Spirit. God had already saved me, but I wanted all that God had for me, including the Holy Spirit. I went forward for prayer. The evangelist and a few other men placed their hands on me and began to pray for me. Soon I was filled with the Holy Spirit and began to speak in tongues! There was an incredible sense of God's presence; I knew it was just the beginning for me.

You should ask God to fill you with the Holy Spirit if you want Him to bring comfort and guide you. Everyone's experience is different. You don't need podcasts, a revival service, or people laying hands on you to receive the Holy Spirit—although those things are great! You just need to pray and ask God for it. The Bible gives numerous examples of people who were filled with the Holy Spirit: Peter and John prayed and laid hands on the Samaritan believers, and they were filled with the Holy Spirit (Acts 8:17); a Roman soldier named Cornelius and his household were filled with the Holy Spirit while Peter was preaching to them (Acts 10:44); and the Ephesian believers who had been baptized in water by John but did not receive the infilling of the Holy Spirit until Paul laid his hands on them (Acts 19:6).

Jesus tells us how to be filled with the Spirit (John 7:37-39)

The first requirement to being filled with the Holy Spirit is to be thirsty. Have you ever been working outside, jogging, or doing some other activity on a hot day and didn't have any water? Your lips and throat became so dry you would have given anything for something cold to drink. As your body began to lose liquid through sweat, your internal need for water began to increase. That is a physical thirst. The systems of being thirsty spiritually are when you realize there is a void, emptiness, restlessness, or you are living an unsatisfied life. So, if you desire to receive the gift of the Holy Spirit, there has to be an intense thirst for God. David had that kind of thirst (Psalm 42:1-2). It all begins with a thirst for God. Thirst for God can be developed by reading the Bible and praying. You can also ask God for a thirst or hang around people who are full of God.

Secondly, Jesus said we had to go to Him (John 7:37). John the Baptist also said Jesus is the one who baptizes in the Holy Spirit (Matt. 3:11). It is not man who fills with the Holy Spirit, but God who uses a variety of people to help those who want to be filled. It could be a pastor, evangelist, deacon, church member, or friend who prays for someone to be filled with the Holy Spirit. The Apostle Paul laid hands on the Ephesian believers and they were filled with the Holy Spirit (Acts 19:6).

The third requirement to being filled with the Holy Spirit is to drink, and by this, I mean praising and seeking God (John 7:37). I have witnessed many believers being filled with the Holy Spirit, but I have also seen some who weren't filled because they did not understand what it meant to drink. Sincere Christians have told me God would have to make them speak in tongues; they would stand there and refuse to open their mouths and refuse to utter a single word. However, we must be willing to open our mouths so that God can speak through us. We have to do the speaking as the Spirit of God gives the utterance (Acts 2:4).

Speaking in tongues is a supernatural utterance by the Holy Spirit in a language never learned by the speaker and is unknown to them. I've heard some people who were filled with the Holy Spirit speak in tongues that sounded like they were speaking fluent Spanish, while others would only speak one syllable in an unknown tongue. At first it may sound odd or even startle you when you start speaking in tongues. No matter what you feel or think, it is God giving you a prayer language. Jesus described it as rivers of living water coming out of your belly or inner being (John 7:38). Remember, God is not going to make you speak; you have to do the speaking.

The last requirement Jesus asked of us to be filled with the Holy Spirit was to believe (John 7:39). When we receive Jesus as our savior, we do it by faith (Eph. 2:8). The same is true with being filled with the Holy Spirit; we receive by faith. The only way we can please God and receive from Him is by faith (Heb. 11:6). At times all of us need help with our disbelief. In Mark 9, we read about a father with a son who was demon possessed. The father had taken his son to the disciples to cast out the devil, but they could not. I'm sure this father was broken-hearted and did not know what to do to help his son. The father took his son to Jesus and He said, "all things are possible to him that believe." The dad responded by saying, "I believe; help thou mine unbelief." No matter what you feel, think, or hear about the infilling of the Holy Spirit and speaking in tongues—believe that you receive.

Why Do We Need the Holy Spirit?

The Holy Spirit helps us to pray (Romans 8:26-

27)

Jesus is in heaven as our high priest praying for us (Romans 8:34), but we also have the Holy Spirit praying for us here on earth (Romans 8:26). We have Jesus and the Holy Spirit praying for us. There will be times when you will not know how or what to pray, but the Holy Spirit will help you. The Holy Spirit does this by interceding with groaning sounds. These audible sounds are given by the Holy Spirit but spoken by an individual. When a believer prays in tongues or worships in tongues it's not for interpretation. When a believer is filled with the Holy Spirit and they pray or worship in tongues, it is his or her spirit praying to God. When the gift of tongues is in operation it is the reverse; it is not man speaking to God, but God speaking to man through a believer. This is called diversities of tongues (1 Corinthians 12:28). God has given you the Holy Spirit to help you pray.

The Holy Spirit gives us power (Acts 1:8)

Walking through this life without the power of the Holy Spirit is like a soldier going into battle without a weapon—it is unwise and unnecessary. God desires to give us his Spirit. We cannot be an effective witness or live for God without the power of the Holy Spirit. The Apostle Peter's life was inconsistent before he was filled with the Holy Spirit. At times he lied, cursed, forsook Jesus, and was a very prideful person—

and that's after he was following Jesus! However, after he was filled with the Holy Spirit, he was a changed man. His life drastically changed for the better. Peter lived a life dedicated to God and became a great witness for the faith. On the day of Pentecost, he preached one of the most powerful messages ever recorded in scriptures— 3,000 people were saved (Act 2:41). If you need help witnessing and living for God, ask Him to fill you with the power of the Holy Spirit.

The Holy Spirit teaches us (John 14:26)

Jesus was the greatest teacher of all time. He captivated the hearts of people with His teachings about life, family, God, heaven, hell, and eternity. The poor, the blind, the lame, and the outcast were drawn to Him because His teachings brought them hope, salvation, healing, and understanding about God's love. Jesus' teachings were given with authority (Matthew 7:28-29), were incomparable (John 7:46), and were gracious (Luke 4:22). He told His followers that when He left the Earth, He would send the Holy Spirit to teach them in His place. In addition to teaching, He sent the Holy Spirit to bring to their remembrance all the things He had said to them (John 14:26). The Holy Spirit is here today to help teach you the word of God and the spiritual things of God (1 Cor. 2:11-13).

God's help through the person of the Holy Spirit is reaching out to you today. Maybe you feel lonely, abandoned, confused, or tired of living in sin. No matter how bad your situation may be, God has sent the Holy Spirit to help you. The Holy Spirit will help comfort you, guide you, help you to pray, give you power, and teach you. It's my prayer for you that God will help guide you as you continue to read each page of this book. You may need guidance in a relationship, job, finances, or career. Let God guide you (Psalm 32:8).

Remember, help is always closer than you think.

Discussion questions:

1. How is the Holy Spirit like God and Jesus?

2. Should we let our conscience guide us?

3. When do we have our first encounter with the Holy Spirit?

4. Should believers be filled with the Holy Spirit?

5. What are some of the ways the Holy Spirit can help you?

2
GOD'S WORD

It would be years later in a Bill Gothard Conference in Memphis before I would receive the help I needed to overcome my dad's death. By this time, I was 26 years old, and it had already been 17 years since my father passed away. I had a very difficult time coping with his death during my childhood years. When I was a little boy, I saw other children at ballgames with their dads, and I felt cheated. My friends at school would talk about their dads taking them fishing, hunting, or just hanging out with them. My dad wasn't there to be with me. Even in my adult years, I was filled with constant reminders of my dad's death and still carried the pain of not seeing or talking to him.

Reverend Gothard spoke about God being a father of the fatherless (Psalm 68:5). While he was reading those verses, I begin to sob and shake uncontrollably in the service. There were hundreds of ministers and lay people all around me, but I could not stop sobbing. At that very moment God's word healed me of all the pain I had held on to over my father's death. I also realized that not only did I have a father, but also a Heavenly Father who loved me and had always been with me. Finally, the pain of not having a father was being taken away.

It was God's word which helped me move past my father's death and fill the tremendous void I had in my life. I have never felt the pain and sorrow of his passing since that day. God's word is a helper to the hurting, and His word will help you in your time of bereavement. Let God's word heal you of the sorrow, loneliness, and pain you may be experiencing today of someone who has passed away. It could be a family member or a longtime friend. His word can bring healing and comfort.

God's word helps us to overcome temptation

It's amazing to hear the different beliefs some people have concerning temptation. Some believe every time they are tempted, they have to commit the act of sin. This is simply not true. There are those who believe you have to sin a little bit every day. Some believe you can live in sin and not worry about the consequences of sin because a loving God would not send you to hell.

Temptation is not a sin. Everyone is tempted. Even Jesus was tempted while He was here on Earth but never sinned (Hebrews 4:15). Temptation becomes sin when we yield or give into the temptation (James 1:14-15).

What does the Bible say about temptation, and how do I use God's word to help me overcome temptation? A great example of overcoming temptation can be found in Matthew chapter four where Jesus is tempted by the devil three times. Jesus had been fasting for 40 days and 40 nights when the devil came and tempted Him. In the first temptation, the devil wanted Jesus to use His divine power to turn stones into bread to meet His physical needs.

Jesus would have sinned if He had turned the stones into bread. First, it would have meant that Jesus did not look to His Father to provide for Him, and secondly that He did not need spiritual nourishment. Too many times we put our physical needs over our spiritual needs. What did Jesus do? He said, "Man shall not live by bread alone, but by every word that proceeds from the mouth of the Lord" (Deu. 8:3).

God is our provider (Matthew 6:30-33), and God's word is life and health to us (Pro. 4:20-22). It's very important for every believer to read, meditate, know, and be able to quote God's word. The devil will try to tempt you into believing you do not need spiritual nourishment and God is not your provider.

In the second temptation, Satan takes Jesus, places Him on the pinnacle of the temple, and tells Him to cast Himself down (Matthew 4:5-7). Satan misquotes the scriptures. He tells Jesus to cast Himself down because God had promised to take care of His own (Psalm 91:11-12). Satan omits the phrase "to keep you in all your ways" and adds "at any time."

Don't think for a minute that the devil will not tempt you at church, the temple, or the synagogue with false doctrine, lies, or with other temptations. If Satan took Jesus to the temple and tempted Him how much more will Satan tempt us at our place of worship? We should never tempt the Lord by deliberately putting ourselves in a threatening or evil situation and then expecting Him to deliver us. God cannot be tempted by evil (James 1:13). Jesus responded by saying we are not to tempt God (Deu. 6:16).

In the third temptation, Satan tempts Jesus by asking Him to worship him in exchange for all the kingdoms of the world (Matthew 4:8-9). Jesus would have sinned if He had bowed down and worshipped the devil. We are only to worship God and nothing else (Exodus 34:14). The devil will do all he can to keep you from worshipping God. You may think there is no way you would worship the devil, but there are many things you could worship without realizing. The question is this—What do I focus on most of the time? Is it success, money, music, sports, a person, friends, my job, or family?   There is nothing wrong with any of these things as long as they are kept in the right perspective. They become sin when we love them more than we do God. Because of Jesus' sinless life and being faithful unto His death on the cross, He is able to help us through His word when we are tempted (Hebrews 2:17-18).

God has always provided a way to escape temptation (1 Cor. 10:13). God's word will not return void (Isaiah 55:11), God's word will not pass away (Mathew 24:35), God's word feeds our soul (Ps. 119:103), God's word help's us to grow spiritually (1 Peter 2:2), God's word lives forever (1 Peter 1:23) God's word furnishes light (Psalm 119:105), and God's word is powerful (Jeremiah 23:29).

God's word helps us to receive healing

During a routine eye exam, I was told I had a tumor in my right eye which resulted in losing some of my vision in that eye. You can't even imagine the emotions I felt after hearing those words. Not being satisfied with that report, I went to another eye doctor who confirmed what the previous test had shown.   But something miraculous happened—a few months later while I was in the process of having various tests done, God healed me. One Sunday morning, my mother-in-law went forward in a church service to pray for me. She believed that God would heal me through His word. She was a very godly lady—full of God's word, faith, and love. God healed me of the tumor, and the only evidence of it ever existing is a blind spot in my eye.

There is power in the written and spoken word of God. We should recognize and use this power. In Mathew chapter 8, there is a story about a Roman centurion who had a servant who was paralyzed. He went to Jesus seeking help. Jesus said he would go and heal the servant.

The centurion responded by saying he was not worthy for Jesus to come to his house but to only speak a word so his servant would be healed. The centurion was a soldier under authority, and when he gave commands they were obeyed. He recognized the authority that Jesus had under God and all that He had to do was to speak and his servant would be healed. His servant was healed within the hour. That same authority has been given to believers (Matthew 18:18).

God's word is life and health to us (Proverbs 4:20-22), God's word heals and delivers (Psalm 107:20), God is watching over His word to perform it (Jeremiah 1:12), faith comes by God's word (Rom. 10:17), and Jesus suffered bodily beatings for our healing (1 Peter 2:24).

God's word helps to hold everything together

At times it seems we are living in a world which is falling apart. Tragically you hear of families who are falling apart because of their job situation, finances, problems at school, health issues or just life in general. Sometimes it gets so bad people will respond by saying they are about to lose their mind.

God's word helps to hold everything together. In Eph. 6 the Apostle Paul names 6 pieces of spiritual armor that a believer should put on every day. In that list of armor, he begins with the word of God and ends with the word of God. We are to put on the belt of truth, the breastplate of righteousness, have our feet shod with the gospel of peace, take the shield of faith, put on the helmet of salvation, and take the sword of the spirit which is the word of God.

In the Apostle Paul's time, Roman soldiers wore a loin belt. His belt held a scabbard for a sword, a pouch that carried his arrows, and his breastplate was attached to it. A soldier's loin belt helped him. It was a valuable piece of armor he needed to hold the other parts of his armor and to protect him.

God has given us His word to help us keep everything together. We have to stand everyday with our loins girded with God's word to receive that help (Eph. 6:14). God's word is that truth we need to wear (John 17:17). God's word is alive, powerful, and sharper than any sword. It pierces and discerns (Heb. 4:12).

According to God's word, positive words bring re wards (Psalm 37:30-33), edify (2 Cor. 12:19), heal (Prov. 12:18), and preserve life (Prov. 18:21). Negative words can result in bad consequences (James 3:5-8), bring evil (Prov. 17:20), and trouble (Psalm 10:7).

God's word has the power to remove the stains of sin

Many of us have experienced times when we were either working on a messy project, spilled a drink on ourselves, or were doing some type of chores and got a bad stain on our clothes. Sometimes the stain was so bad the garment could not be cleaned and had to be disregarded or used for rags.

Over the years, I have met people who believe their sins were so great they could not be forgiven. Some felt they were doomed to die separated from God. There is only one sin that man cannot be forgiven for and that is blasphemy against the Holy Spirit (Matthew 12:31). This means someone has said the work of the Holy Spirit is the work of the devil.

There is not one sin, spot, or stain in our lives that the word of God and the blood of Jesus cannot remove. The word of God sanctifies, cleanses, removes spots, removes wrinkles, and removes blemishes (Eph. 5:26-27). God's word has the power to remove all the stains of sin.

Remember, help is always closer than you think.

Discussion questions:

1. Is temptation a sin?

2. What is the Biblical way to respond to temptation?

3. How can I increase my faith?

4. What is the only sin we cannot be forgiven for?

5. Name at least four attributes of God's word.

3

ANGELS

It was on a Sunday morning when I received the heart-breaking news my mother-in-law, Mary, did not have much longer to live. She was already on hospice. Early that morning, a nurse told a family member she needed to call family in because it wouldn't be long before she passed away. I was in Knoxville, which was four hours away, and I wanted desperately to see her before she passed away. I loved Mary dearly and wanted to be by her bedside in her last hours. She helped lead me to the Lord, helped me grow in the Lord, constantly prayed for me, and loved me like a son. Now it looked like I wouldn't be with her in her final moments before she went to heaven.

I turned on my emergency flashers and headed to Lexington, Tennessee as fast as I could. During the course of driving there, one of my sisters-in-law thought Mary was waiting for me before she would let go. A nurse told the family that it could be the reason why she was hanging on. Her condition was deteriorating with every passing minute. They called me to tell me what my sister-in-law and the nurse had said. Even though Mary wasn't conscious, I told them to tell her I was on my way and how close I was getting. It was my belief she could hear them even though she was not responding. I called the family to update them when I was two hours away, when I was one hour away, and then finally when I arrived at the nursing home.

When I walked into the room and saw Mary, I was overtaken with grief to see the condition she was in. I told her I sensed there were angels in the room, and it would be ok to slip out. I prayed for her, we sung the chorus of "He Touched Me" twice, and then she passed away. I was thankful to God that I was able to spend the last 10 minutes of her life with her. Our hearts were broken, but we knew Mary had gone on to her eternal reward and the angels were there to help escort her to heaven.

Angels care for God's people at death

Over the years, there have been numerous times as a pastor that I have been summoned to the bedside of precious saints who were on their deathbeds. I've stood at the bedside of dying elderly people who had lived a long life, loved God, loved their family and served the Lord most of their life. Then, there have been times I stood and wept at the bedside of a young person who died unexpectedly and was just starting his or her life. The most difficult time is seeing a newborn or young infant who only lived a few days or weeks. There is always a tremendous sense of sorrow and loss in the room, but many times I have sensed something else there and that was the presence of angels.

I know without question God's word and the Holy Spirit always bring help, comfort, and peace to the broken hearted when there is death. However, there is another source of help present and that is the presence of angels. You may not see or feel them, but many times they are there.

Jesus tells the story of two men who died, and angels were present at the death of one of them (Luke 16:19-31). One man was very rich, and the other man was a poor beggar by the name of Lazarus. The beggar was placed at the gate of the rich man because he desired to eat the crumbs that fell from the rich man's table. His body was covered with sores, and dogs would come to lick his sores. Lazarus had a horrible life but when he died, he had angels to carry him to paradise (Luke 16:22). There is no mention of angels carrying the rich man to his reward which was eternal torment and separation from God.

Death is mysterious and is approached by many with great fear. I'm thankful to God, because of His great love He sends angels to take believers to heaven. Angels are Gods' helpers. The next time you're at the bedside of a loved one who is about to depart this life or when you're at death's door and in great sorrow, look around. There may be angels present to help minister to them and you (Heb. 1:14).

Angels destroy the enemies of God

In Matthew 26:47, we read that a multitude of soldiers came to arrest Jesus in the Garden of Gethsemane. One of His disciples, Judas Iscariot, betrayed Jesus for 30 pieces of silver. He led the religious leaders and soldiers to where Jesus was praying with some of His other disciples. One of those disciples with Jesus was Peter who pulled out a sword to fight the soldiers. Jesus told Peter to put away his sword because He could pray to His Father who would send more than 12 legions of angels to help Him. A legion consisted of 6,000 men. That meant God could send Jesus more than 72,000 angels to rescue Him. Jesus refused any help and submitted to being arrested to fulfill the plan of salvation for all mankind.

We read that God once used a single angel to destroy 185,000 Assyrians (Isa. 37:36). If God had sent Jesus those or 72,000 angels to help Him, based on the example of one angel destroying 185,000 men, 12 legions would have the capacity of destroying 13,320,000,000 of His enemies. Angels cast the devil and his angels out of heaven (Rev. 12:7-9). An angel will cast the devil into the bottomless pit for a thousand years (Rev. 20:1-3). Angels helped God destroy His enemies.

In 2 Kings chapter 6, the king of Syria dispatched a large army to surround the prophet Elisha and the children of Israel. Their situation looked hopeless. The king of Syria had been told no one would fight with Israel, but he did not know God would fight for them. Early the next morning Elisha's servant went and saw the huge Syrian army which surrounded them and the whole city. Elisha's servant had no faith. There are all kinds of evil at work against us. We are surrounded by the host of hell because Satan is out to destroy us (John 10:10). Elisha's servant went and told Elisha about the huge army. Elisha prayed God would open his servant's eyes to not only see the problem but the solution. The servant's eyes were opened, and he saw their enemies were surrounded by angels far more powerful than any earthly army (2 Kings 6:16). I pray in every insurmountable situation we face that we would realize the spiritual forces God has provided for us to surround the enemies who surround us.

Angels protect God's people

Several years ago, my wife and I took our

sons to an amusement park in Hot Spring, Arkansas. Once inside the park, we were making our way to the ferris wheel when the Holy Spirit said to me "do not let your children ride the Ferris wheel." He didn't say why but just said not to let them ride it. I didn't tell my sons what the Holy Spirit had said to me but only that they could not ride the Ferris wheel.

There are times the Holy Spirit speaks to us to keep us from harm. Once the ride started, something mechanically broke which hindered the ferris wheel from coming to a complete stop. The people on the ride began to realize something was wrong and began to panic. After a short time, some workers arrived to try to make the necessary repairs, but it seemed like there was not much progress being made. I remember walking away from everyone and thanking the Lord for sparing my sons from the horror of what was happening and then I said, "but what about all the other children and parents who were on the ride that needed help?" I'm convinced God sent an angel to help. While the Ferris wheel could not come to a complete stop, all the passengers were safely unloaded.

Daniel was a godly man in the Old Testament who prayed constantly, had visions, received great revelations from God, and was protected from lions by an angel. There were men in the time of Daniel who were very jealous of him. They sought ways to have him arrested and even killed.

These men had the king decree no man could pray to any god or man except the king for 30 days. They knew Daniel prayed three times daily to God, and he would be thrown into the lion's den for violating the decree. Daniel was arrested and thrown into the lions' den, but he was protected by an angel from God (Daniel 6:19-22). Only eternity will reveal the times angels have helped to protect us in this life.

Angels take on human form

People have all kinds of ideas about what angels look like. In the movie, "It's a Wonderful Life," an angel named Clarence appears as an old man who rescues George Bailey when he is suicidal. At the end of the movie, his daughter hears a bell ring and tells her father that her teacher said, "every time a bell rings an angel gets his wings." While that was a very moving part of the movie, angels do not earn their wings. Angels can take on human form and even appear to us, but we may not even be aware of it (Heb. 13:2). An angel appeared to Daniel (Daniel 8:15) and to Cornelius (Acts 10:30). These angels appeared as men. The next knock on your door could be an angel sent by God to help you. I wonder how many times we have received an angelic visit from God and not even realized it.

Angels deliver messages

From the beginning of time, man has developed various ways to send messages. Some of the earliest messages were sent on parchment, carved stone, drums, smoke signals, pigeons, pony express, and the Postal Service. As time went on the telegraph and phone were invented to communicate and send messages. In recent years, we have e-mail, Facebook, Instagram, Twitter, Snapchat, along with other numerous ways to send and receive messages. There is a message system that has been around before creation that is far more reliable then man's inventions and that is God's angels. Angels obey the commands of God to deliver messages when instructed (Psalm 103:20). God's angels deliver messages to His people.

An angel was sent to Daniel who had been struggling in prayer for 21 days over the interpretation of a dream he had (Daniel 10:1-14). On the 21st day, an angel came to Daniel and said the prince of the kingdom of Persia had hindered him but Michael, one of the chief princes, came and helped him. The angels helped Daniel by delivering the interpretation to him. Some Christians would have a difficult time praying over one need for 21 days. Jesus told us to continue praying and not to stop until the answer comes (Luke 11:9-10). An angel could be assigned by God to help bring the answer.

An angel delivered a message to Samson's mother (Judges 13:3), to Joseph (Matt. 1:20-23), to

Mary the mother of Jesus (Luke 1:26-37), to the disciples at the ascension of Jesus (Acts 1:9-11), to Philip (Acts 8:26), and to Cornelius (Acts 10:3-6). There are numerous places in the Bible where God sent an angel to deliver messages.

Angels fill heaven and earth with praise

Have you ever been to a ballgame, rock concert, or an event where the noise level was extremely deafening? Many of us have at some point and time. To little children, it can be frightening. An angel announced the birth of Jesus to shepherds while attending their sheep (Luke 2:8-14). The announcement about the birth from an angel came without any warning and was followed by a great heavenly host of angels praising God. I can't imagine what went through the shepherds' minds when a multitude of angels begin to praise God over the birth of Jesus. Angels in great number are around the throne of God constantly praising God (Rev. 5:11-12).

Remember, help is always closer than you think.

Discussion questions:

1. Can angels take on human form? Give scripture reference.

2. Give a scripture reference that angels

escort believers to heaven.

3. Do angels deliver messages? Give three examples.

4. Has there been a time you knew that God had sent an angel to help you?

5. What are angels doing around the throne room?

4

FAITH

In 1984, I was pastoring First Assembly of
God in Horn Lake, Mississippi and heard about a
church that was without a pastor in central
Mississippi. I begin to pray about God's direction
for my life and whether or not I should submit a
resume to the church for the possibility of
becoming its pastor. If God led me there, I would
need to resign the church I was currently
pastoring and a full-time job as well. I had been a
bi-vocational pastor for several years, and this
would be a huge step of faith for me and my
family. Before meeting with the church board
and congregation, I drove to the city to pray and
look the city over. While there, God spoke to my
heart, "this is the city I want you to pastor." A
few days later, I called the District
Superintendent and shared with him how I felt
God calling me to the area, and I was going to
submit a resume to the church board. He told me

this particular church was a good church, but many of its previous pastors had not had long tenures there.

Several weeks later I would have the privilege of meeting with the wonderful people of the church, the church board, the youth department, Sunday School teachers, and the women's department. I also preached Saturday night and two services Sunday. Following the Sunday night service, the church would vote to decide whether they wanted me to be their pastor. It required two-thirds vote for me to be elected, and I came up one vote shy of the mark. That night, my family and I told the church families good-bye and drove back home.

The next morning, I went into a time of prayer feeling somewhat confused and hurt that I was not elected, especially after what God had spoken to me about pastoring in that particular city. I held on to faith and refused to let my feelings be the enemy of my faith. We are to walk by faith, not sight (2 Cor. 5:7). After much prayer and continuing in faith, a few weeks later the church voted again, and they elected me to be their pastor. Without God's help of bringing the people together and the church having another vote, I would not have been elected as pastor. I had the great privilege of pastoring there for four and half years and saw God do some wonderful works there.

Faith is another helper from God which can help you during your most difficult times and seemly impossible situations. You may not be a pastor who is seeking God's will for ministry, but there could be areas of your life God has spoken to you about that have not come to pass yet. Hold on to faith. To overcome the world and walk in victory, you must have faith (1 John 5:4). We cannot get saved without having faith (Eph. 2:8). God has given every born-again person a measure of faith (Romans 12:3). We receive more faith by reading the word of God (Rom. 10:17). It is impossible to please God without faith (Heb. 11:6).

If you continue in faith God will reward you for your consistent walk and life of faith (Heb. 10:35). Too many people give up or quit when they are just on the brink of a miracle or an answer to a prayer.

Why is it that some people just give up or quit? There are enemies of our faith. These enemies of faith will stop you in your tracks. In this chapter let's look at three enemies of our faith:

Our Thought Life

What we think in our mind and heart is what we become (Pro. 23:7). In other words, a man is what he thinks. Your mind is like a computer that is always taking in the information fed into it. Everything that is loaded or fed onto your office or home computer stays there unless you delete it. Your mind is the same way. We have to be very careful what we put in our minds. If we are not careful, our thought life can become the enemy of our faith by the things we feed into it.

So, the question is this—what feeds our mind? One thing that feeds our mind is our five senses. A lot of what you have learned since childbirth has come through your five senses. Some good and some bad. Our minds should be filled with God's word everyday by reading and meditating on it. God's word gives us stability, fruitfulness, and prosperousness when we read His word (Psalm 1:2-3). I know some people who listen to Christian music or the Bible while sleeping. They are feeding their thought life with positive things even while they are sleeping. The great Apostle Paul said to think on things that are true, honest, just, pure, lovely, good report, things that have virtue, and that are praiseworthy (Phil. 4:8).

The devil can feed your thought life by bombarding your mind with bad thoughts. Those bad or evil thoughts are not sin unless you act on them. The devil put into the heart or mind of Judas Iscariot to betray Jesus (John 13:2). It started with Judas' thought life. We should cast bad thoughts or imaginations down (2 Cor. 10:5). Satan cannot read your mind, but he will attack your mind and try to fill it with negative things. Adam and Eve—through evil thoughts by the devil—disobeyed God and, because of their disobedience, sin entered the world (Gen. 3:6).

There is help for your thought life. Choose to have your mind renewed every day instead of being conformed to the world (Rom. 12:2), choose to be spiritually minded instead of carnally minded (Rom. 8:6), and choose to not be double minded (James 1:5-8). Our thought life can be the enemy of our faith. God has given you faith to help you, but don't let bad or negative thoughts rob you of what God has for you.

Weariness

Weariness is an enemy of your faith. No one is exempt from becoming weary. Rebekah, the wife of Isaac, became weary (Gen. 27:46), Job became weary (Job 10:1), and even King David, a man after God's own heart, became weary (Psalm 6:6). The Apostle Paul said for us not to become weary in well doing (Gal. 6:9). People become weary by working long hours, bill paying, family problems, health issues, and even weary of life in general. The devil comes to us when we are weary. If you become weary in your faith you will not be able to stand against the devil when he attacks you, your family, or home.

Peter said for us to humble ourselves by submitting to God and to cast every care on Him because the devil is going about as a roaring lion seeking whomever he may devour (1 Peter 5:6-8). It's okay to say to God, "this is more than I can handle." Give God all your cares and junk. He is the best junk man you will ever find—even better than Fred Sanford. Don't become faithless through weariness. Wait on God, and He will renew your strength (Isa. 40:31). Don't let weariness cause you to lose faith.

Unbelief

Unbelief is another enemy of our faith. Unbelief is opposite of faith and according to God's word is sin (Rom. 14:23). God has given you faith to help you, but unbelief will hinder you from receiving God's help. God wants to help you, but help is received when we act and move in faith.

In Matthew 14:22, Jesus told His disciples to get in a boat and sail to the other side of the sea. Before they could reach land, a horrible storm came up. Storms were not new to some of the disciples as they were experienced fishermen and had been caught in storms before. Remember— the disciples were only doing what Jesus told them to do. Sometimes major storms are going to come while you are doing the will of God. Don't let unbelief come in and shake your faith but hold fast to your faith. While the storm was raging, Jesus came to His disciples by walking on the water. The disciples were very fearful thinking it was a spirit they were seeing and cried out with fear. Jesus told them to not be afraid, be of good cheer, and that it was Him. Peter said,

"Lord, if it's you, command me to come on the water to where you are." Peter stepped out of boat and walked on the raging water until he got his eyes off of Jesus and onto the storm. By faith Peter walked on the water until unbelief came in and he began to sink. Jesus reached out His hand and saved Peter from drowning.

Your storm may come suddenly and without warning but keep your eyes on Jesus who is the author and finisher of your faith (Heb. 12:2). Remember God has given everyone the measure of faith (Rom.12:3); God even blesses those who only have mustard seed faith (Matt. 17:20); and Jesus recognized two people who had great faith—a centurion (Matt. 8:5-10) and a woman with a demon possessed daughter had great faith (Matt. 15:21-28). This woman's great faith is seen by several things. First, she did not let the rejection of Jesus and the disciples stop her. Can you imagine that Jesus would not respond to the cries of a helpless Mother whose child was demon possessed? He ignored her. Even the disciples were against her and said, "Send her away. She's bothering us." Now, she is told by Jesus that He is only sent to the house of Israel which did not include her because she was a Canaanite-an enemy of the Israelites. At that point, most people would have left Jesus with their prayers unanswered and still in need of help. To make matters even worse, Jesus compared her to a dog. This dear mom believed that she had the right to receive help from the hand of God. Through her faith her daughter was delivered.

The disciples had no faith when caught in another storm with Jesus in the boat with them (Mark 4:40). Jesus prayed for Peter that his faith would not fail (Luke 22:32).

Don't let your thought life, weariness, or unbelief hinder you from receiving God's help.

Remember, help is always closer than you think.

Discussion questions:

1. Can my thought life effect my faith in a negative way? If so, how?

2. What can I do to protect my thought life?

3. Name two people that Jesus said had "great" faith.

4. How does faith relate to salvation?

5. Can your faith help someone else receive an answer to prayer?

5

THE NAME OF JESUS

A 17-year-old girl who was a third-generation witch called a church in Evansville, Indiana from a bus station where my son, Jon, served as youth pastor. She shared with the church secretary that she had been told all her life she would be sacrificed on her 17th birthday which was that very day. She was in Evansville with her family and other members of a cult group to hand out free tickets to a concert held later in the week. The reason for the free tickets was to encourage people to attend the concert where an invitation would be given to join the church of Satan.

It was decided that my son and the church secretary would go and bring the girl to the church. Upon arriving at the church, the girl refused to go inside. When asked why, she said she had been told all of her life that if she ever went into a building that had a cross on it, she would die. After much persuasion, she went inside the church sanctuary where believers prayed for her for several hours. Eight demons were cast out of this 17-year-old teenager. Each demon had a distinct personality, that spoke with different voices, and manifested violent behavior when cast out. This demon-possessed teenager received God's help by the power that is in the name of Jesus. God has given us the name of Jesus to help us to cast out devils.

People who are demon possessed will not be delivered by some religious ceremony or magical formula but by the power that is in the name of Jesus. Seven unbelieving brothers tried to cast out an evil spirit, but instead of casting out the demon, the brothers were overcome and stripped of their clothing by the evil spirit (Acts 19:14-16). Dealing with demon-possessed people is a very serious matter and should be done by Spirit-filled believers (Acts 1:8).

Jesus told His disciples to cast out devils in His name (Mark 16:17). Jesus cast devils out of Mary Magdalene (Luke 8:2), out of a man who lived in the tombs (Luke 8:27), and many other people that were brought to Him (Matt. 8:16).

The Apostle Paul cast a devil out of a young lady who was a fortune teller (Acts 16:18). Remember—the only way demons can be cast out is by invoking the power that is in the name of Jesus prayed by Spirit-filled believers. There is not any name that has been given to anyone that is above the name of Jesus (Phil. 2:9).

Pray in the name of Jesus

Over the last several years, we have been inundated with teachings on prayer. Many mainline denominations teach on prayer, have prayer during their services, and even encourage their members to pray daily. Numerous books have been written recently on how to pray, when to pray, where to pray, and what to pray. Prayer should be a part of every believer's life. Is there a right way and a wrong way to pray? Yes. Jesus gives us the most defined teachings on prayer and how to pray in the gospels. Jesus said to go into your prayer closet and pray to the Father (Matt. 6:6), to pray in His name (John 14:13), that we should always pray (Luke 18:1), and pray that we not enter into temptation (Matt. 26:41). God will help you when you pray to the Father in the name of Jesus.

Praying "in Jesus' name" is more than just a phrase to open or close out a prayer. It means we are praying according to His nature, His heart, and by His authority. All that we need or ever hope for is found in Jesus. He is the bread of life (John 6:48); the way, truth, and life (John 14:6); the door (John 10:9), the light of the world (John 8:12); and the good shepherd (John 10:14).

Paul told Timothy to pray lifting up holy hands without wrath and doubting (1 Tim. 2:8). Many parents teach their children to fold their hands and close their eyes. I'm not saying that is a wrong way to pray, but we do not see that taught in the scriptures. I'm convinced it's not the position of the body when we are praying but the position of the heart. You can pray while walking, kneeling at an altar, or laying on the floor, but the most important thing to do is to pray with a pure heart.

Praying to our Heavenly Father in the name of Jesus brings us to a place of closeness and intimacy with God who longs for us to come and be face to face with Him. God wants to help you, but you have to go to Him in prayer in the name of Jesus.

Assemble in the name of Jesus

I have been in church services, Bible studies, cell groups, and church outings where the name of Jesus was never mentioned. What a sad indictment against the church and believers. Jesus said He would be in our midst when we gather in His name (Matt. 18:20). How can we expect God to help us when we meet for services, pray, or have any church activity when we don't assemble in His name? The Apostle Paul said whatever we do in word or deed we should do in the name of the Lord Jesus (Col. 3:17). Any church service or church activity without assembling in the name of the Lord is just another meeting that doesn't see any lives changed or encouraged. God desires to help us when we assemble with other believers, but we must gather in the name of Jesus to receive His help.

Healing in the name of Jesus

In Old Testament times, God was identified by His covenant names. All of these covenant names were very powerful and revealed who He was. Each name was given to help us in our relationship, our walk, and to have a better understanding of His character. One of God's Old Testament covenant names was Jehovah-Rapha which means the Lord that heals, to make whole, or repair (Ex. 15:26).

Healing is provided for us through the brutal beatings Jesus took before He died on the cross. In fact, His suffering was predicted and promised in the Old Testament years before Christ came (Isa. 53:5). Matt. 27:26 tells us Pilate "had scourged Jesus" before He was crucified. Jesus was stripped down and shackled to a post with His hands secured over His head. A Roman soldier took a wooden whip that had 12- to 24-inch long straps with pieces of sharp glass, bone fragments, or pieces of metal attached to it. This means of punishment was so torturous that it would pull the flesh off of its victims back exposing bones and muscles. Those being scourged were given 39 lashes and some died from the massive beating. Jesus was probably unrecognizable after the severe beating, bleeding, and bruising.

Peter quotes Isa. 53:5 "...by whose stripes ye were healed" (1 Peter 2:24). Jesus' body was brutally beaten for us to have bodily healing. In Mark 16:18, Jesus told His followers to lay hands on the sick in His name and that they would recover. There is healing in the name of Jesus.

Receive a little child in the name of Jesus

Jesus said when we receive or welcome a little child in His name, it would be as if we were receiving or welcoming Him (Matt. 18:5). During Jesus' earthly ministry, parents brought their children to Him for prayer (Matt. 19:13). His disciples rebuked the parents, but Jesus made it clear to let the children come to Him. Our world today does not see the importance of children receiving the teachings, love, and touch of Jesus as well. Many children are abused, neglected, and unloved that need to be received by someone who represents Christ.

You may be a Sunday School teacher, children's church volunteer, pastor, nursery worker, or just a neighbor to children who need to be received. Who knows—that little child in your classroom or neighborhood could possibly grow up to be a great preacher such as Billy

Graham, Dwight L. Moody, Charles Wesley, or Charles Spurgeon.

Just remember when you receive a child in the name of Jesus it's the same as receiving Christ.

Stand against the enemies of God

It's hard to imagine but we are in a constant battle against the forces of evil. The Apostle Paul describes this evil as principalities, powers, rulers of the darkness of this world, and spiritual wickedness in high places (Eph. 6:12). Paul made it clear that we are not fighting against flesh and blood. Life is not a playground but a battleground. One of the reasons so many believers are weak and struggling is because they are not dressed for warfare. They have on their Sunday go-to- meeting clothes and have forgot to put on the armor of God.

We are to stand with our loins girted with the truth of God's word, which will protect the private life of our spiritual man; our chest covered with the breastplate of righteousness, which means doing right; our feet shod with the gospel of peace, which means I don't walk on people but share the gospel with people; take up the shield of faith to quench the fiery darts of hell; put on the helmet of salvation to protect our thought life; and to take the sword of the Spirit, which is the word of God, that we will be able to speak at the right time to the right person (Eph. 6:14-17).

Our fleshly and worldly ways of fighting will not help us stand against the enemies of God. David told Goliath, the giant who fought with the Philistines, you come to me with a sword, a spear, and a shield, but I come to you in the name of the Lord (1 Sam. 17:45). David killed Goliath with his slingshot and won a great victory for the children of Israel.

How are you standing? In your own strength or God's? Paul said whatever we do in word or deed to do all in the name of the Lord Jesus (Col. 3:17). The psalmist said our help is in the name of the Lord (Psalm 124:8).

Remember, help is always closer than you think.

Discussion questions:
1. How are demons cast out of people and by whom?

2. What does it mean to pray in Jesus' name?

3. Where did Jesus tell us to go to pray?

4. Name four things the Apostle Paul said we were fighting against?

5. How should we receive little children?

6

THE BLOOD OF JESUS

In December of 2016, my granddaughter's mother was shot multiple times in the head in her home by her business partner to avoid paying back money she had loaned him. My granddaughter was only 6-years-old at the time of her mother's death. I could not even begin to imagine her life without her mother. It would be two years before the case would go to trial. Day after day, I sat in the courtroom listening to attorneys and praying the accused would be found guilty of his horrible crime. The jury deliberated for only one hour and then returned with a guilty verdict. I thought very little about forgiveness for the man who killed my granddaughter's mother. But, deep down on the inside, I knew the same blood that helped me to receive forgiveness would help a convicted murderer to receive forgiveness.

The blood of Jesus is so powerful that the vilest person can be forgiven (Matt. 26:28). It doesn't matter if you are a murderer, thief, robber, rapist, or hardened criminal—the blood of Jesus can and will redeem you (1 Pet. 1:18-19). Without the shedding of blood, there is no salvation (Heb. 9:22).

Numerous songs have been written about the blood of Jesus. Andrae Crouch wrote a powerful song titled, "The Blood Will Never Lose Its Power." Here are some lyrics from that song:

The blood that Jesus shed for me
Way back on Calvary
The blood that gives me strength
From day to day
It will never lose its power
It reaches to the highest mountain
It flows to the lowest valley
The blood that gives me strength
From day to day
It will never lose its power

The words to that song remind us just how powerful the blood of Jesus is. The word "blood" is found 357 times in the Bible. You may be asking—can and how does the blood of Jesus help me in my day-to-day walk with God? The answer is yes it does, and this chapter is dedicated to answering that question.

When the hour is dark, when nothing is externally right, or we are in the dungeon of depression, discouragement, alone and being attacked, we need the blood of Jesus to help us.

The blood at the Passover

The children of Israel were in Egyptian captivity living as slaves under the strong hand and control of the Pharaoh. God sent Moses to the courts of the Pharaoh to demand he let the children of Israel go free. Time after time and plague after plague, Moses would go before the Pharaoh, but he would refuse to let the children of Israel go. The final plague in Egypt, which was the death of all the firstborn children, would cause the Pharaoh to let the children of Israel go. To protect the children of Israel's firstborn from dying, the blood of a lamb had to be applied to every doorpost of the Israelites (Ex. 12:11-30).

The Pharaoh's firstborn son died, and all the firstborn of the Egyptians also died because the blood of a lamb was not applied to their doorpost. This would be the final plague in Egypt before the Pharaoh would let the children of Israel go. The blood alone was not enough to save their families. The children of Israel had to apply the blood to the doorposts of their own homes. When the death angel saw the blood on the doorposts, he would pass over that house. Today, Jesus stands and knocks at the door of our hearts and, just like the blood had to be applied to the doorposts in Egypt, every person must open the door to his own heart to be saved (Rev. 3:20). Jesus' blood needs to be applied every day to our lives.

The blood of Jesus

A 17-year old was arrested for reckless driving in a rural community. As he was brought into court, he was relieved to see his father was the presiding judge. An hour later, the judge rendered his decision. "Your reckless driving," he said, "has endangered the people of our community. Consequently, justice must be served. You will either pay one thousand dollars or serve one year in jail."

"Dad," the boy said, "You know I don't have a penny to my name."

"Young man," said his father, "in this court you will address me as Your Honor. I am your judge." And down went the gavel as the boy stood incredulous before the bench. The bailiff approached. He was ready to take the boy to jail when the judge stood up, took off his robe, and left the bench to stand by his son. "Behind the bench," he said, "I am your judge. But here beside you, I stand as your father." And he took a checkbook from his pocket to pay his son's fine.

That's exactly what Jesus did for us. He left His Father and the splendor of heaven to pay the debt of our sins and the sins of the world by shedding His blood on the cross (Phil. 2:5-8). We have an advocate with the Son, Jesus Christ the righteous, who will stand and defend us (1 John 2:1). Some believe that Jesus was a prophet, but not our Savior, while others believe that He was a good man, but not the Son of God. Jesus is the only way to eternal life (John 14:6). There hast to be repentance towards God, the confessing of Jesus with your mouth, and believing God raised Jesus from the dead to be saved (Rom. 10:9-10). Salvation and eternal life are only made possible by the blood of Jesus and His resurrection from the dead.

There is peace through the blood of the cross (Col. 1:20). This means we are at harmony or in unity with God, with one another and with ourselves. So many families are in confusion, turmoil, and strife. It seems they have anything but peace. God is a God of peace and He desires for us to be at peace with one another (Col. 3:15).

The blood of Jesus justifies us (Rom. 5:9), allows us to go boldly into the throne of God (Heb. 10:19), gives us an everlasting covenant with God (Heb.13:20), provides us with eternal redemption (Heb. 9:12) and purifies us (Heb. 913-14).

Pleading the blood of Jesus

What does it mean to plead the blood? My mother-in-law was the first person I ever heard say, "I plead the blood." One day I walked into her home and she was praying "I plead the blood" over my family. I had never heard that expression before and was somewhat taken back by it. Whether we believe it or not, there are unseen powers we wrestle with from day to day. They are called principalities, powers, rulers of the darkness of this world, and spiritual wickedness in high places (Eph. 6:12). Jesus made it very clear when He said the thief comes to steal, kill, and to destroy (John 10:10). The devil is a liar and the father of all lies (John 8:44).

We are cleansed by the blood of Jesus (1 John 1:7) and overcome by the blood of Jesus (Rev. 12:11). The blood of Jesus has already been shed for our sins, and it is vital that we recognize the power in the blood of Jesus. The devil does not want you to learn about the blood of Jesus, sing about the blood of Jesus, or speak or plead the blood of Jesus. As believers, we should be claiming, speaking, and pleading the blood of Jesus over our families, homes, and when we are attacked.

One night, I received a phone call from one of my students who attended our youth group. He was in the home of another student along with about 20 other students. I could tell from his voice he was extremely upset and shaken. He shared with me that something very evil was manifesting itself in the house where the youth group had gathered. I immediately left my home to go see what was happening with our youth group. Upon arriving, all of the youth were standing in the front yard. Some were crying while others were visibly overwhelmed by what they had seen and heard. The students said there were noises and things moving in the house that could not be explained. Upon entering the house, I knew immediately there was an evil spirit present there. After an hour of pleading the blood and commanding the evil spirit to leave in the name of Jesus, the evil spirit left. I never move into a house without walking around inside and outside pleading the blood of Jesus over it and anointing it with oil.

Some people don't believe that evil spirits can be manifested today. But they still are. There is such an evil in the world today that is causing people to move farther and farther away from God. Many times over the years, I have been summoned to go and pray evil spirits out of peoples' homes. You may be asking, "how does the door open for an evil spirit to come into a home?" It is unbiblical, unwise, and can open the door for an evil spirit to come in by seeking a fortune teller, crystal ball, tarot cards, Ouija board, or anything that is described as divination (2 Chron. 33:6, Lev. 19:31, Gal. 5:20). Entire nations are deceived by the use of sorceries (Rev. 18:3). We are told to seek God (Psalm 70:4), His word (John 5:39), His kingdom (Matt. 6:33), and His will (Matt. 6:10) for our future.

It's imperative a believer be filled with the Holy Spirit and be covered by the blood of Jesus before casting out an evil spirit in someone's home or in an individual. In the Old Testament, Aaron's sons, who were priests, had blood applied to the tips of their right ears, the thumbs of their right hands, and their large toes on their right foot before going into the temple (Lev. 8:24). Why was this done? To cleanse them of the things they had heard, the things they had done, and the places they had gone that had polluted them. Believers today don't have to do that ceremonial cleansing as they did in the Old Testament. However, before we minister, we must plead the blood of Jesus over us to cleanse us and to protect us.

The power in the blood of Jesus

Some of the major nations of this world are constantly trying to develop nuclear weapons to destroy other nations. Their sole purpose is to take control of the entire world. These power-hungry nations have no concerns for bloodshed, death, and destruction. They are controlled by evil forces. This evil can only be broken by the power in the blood of Jesus. The Bible and history books record some of the greatest atrocities that have happened since the beginning of time.

Think of the most despicable person you know. Maybe you know that person personally. Now, imagine that God says the power of His Son's blood is even able to redeem and forgive them (Rev. 1:5). Jesus' blood gives every human being access to the throne room of God (Heb. 10:19). The only requirement is to repent and receive Christ as Lord to have a home in eternity. There is power in the blood of Jesus.

Remember, help is always closer than you think.

Discussion questions:

1. What did the children of Israel do to protect their firstborn from dying in the Passover?

2. How can the blood of Jesus be applied to my life?

3. Can evil spirits manifest today?

4. What does it mean to plead the blood of Jesus?

5. Can the blood of Jesus cleanse a person that has committed horrendous crimes

against families, friends, and loved ones?

7
GOD'S PEOPLE

There was a telegraph company in the 1800's that needed to hire an operator. It would be a great opportunity along with a great salary. Seven men showed up for the interview. They sat outside the boss' office waiting for their interviews and listening to the telegraph operators working in the background. Suddenly, the last one to arrive stood up and went into the boss' office without being asked. The boss came out of his office a few minutes later and said, "Gentlemen, thank you for coming, but there will be no need for an interview. I've hired this man for the position."

One of the remaining six protested saying, "Wait a minute that's not fair. This man was the last to arrive. We should have had our chance to be interviewed for this position."

"You did," the boss said. "While you were sitting here, one of our operators was tapping out a message saying, 'If you receive this message, come into my office immediately. The job is yours.'" All of the men had knowledge of Morse code, but only one of the seven was listening to the message being tapped out right then.

Are you taking the time to listen for the cries for help? There are a lot of people calling out for help, but it seems most are not listening. Cries for help are coming from all walks of life, no matter the status a person has or lack thereof. We need to be God Helpers.

On December 8 at 10:50 p.m., John Lennon—founder of The Beatles—was shot in the back four times as he exited a limousine to go inside his Manhattan residence, The Dakota. He was rushed to Roosevelt Hospital, where he was pronounced dead on arrival at 11 p.m. Lennon wrote numerous songs that referenced peace, drugs, life, love, and hate. One song he wrote with Paul McCartney was titled "Help." It seems John was credited to writing the lyrics as it would be the theme song for The Beatles' second movie, "Help." Lennon was undoubtedly going through something when he penned those words. In a statement he said, "I mean it. It's real! It's just me singing 'Help!' And I meant it...When 'Help' came out, I was crying out for help."

John Lennon was crying out for help, but it

seemed no one heard his pleas.

Depression is a serious medical illness which affects an estimated 16 million American adults. People of all ages deal with depression, and it plays a role in more than one half of all suicide attempts if it goes untreated. Pastor Jarred Wilson of Harvest Christian Fellowship Church committed suicide a few hours after officiating a funeral for a suicide victim. He was only 30 years old at the time. Pastor Wilson was open about his struggle with depression and encouraged others to be open with their depression. Then there are those who don't show any signs of depression outwardly but on the inside are hurting and are calling out for help.

How can I be a God Helper?

Have an encounter with God

In Isaiah chapter 6, we read that after King Uzziah died Isaiah saw a vision of the Lord in His throne room. King Uzziah was well known for walking with the Lord. He brought peace and prosperity to the land. Undoubtedly Isaiah loved the king, but it is interesting to read that it was after Uzziah died that Isaiah saw the Lord in a vision. It's sad to say, but sometimes we don't seek or have an encounter with the Lord until we are experiencing the pain and heartache that comes at the death of a loved one.

There are times when we receive a bad report from the doctor or are just going through a difficult time in our marriage that we finally reach out to the Lord. We shouldn't wait until those times to have an encounter with God. How did Isaiah encounter God? First, he saw the holiness of God and responded by saying, "Woe is me. God is a holy God and desires that we be holy" (1 Peter 1:16). Isaiah's first reaction in the first five chapters of Isaiah were, "Woe unto you. Woe unto you. Woe unto you." But when he saw the holiness of the Lord he said, "Woe is me." We need to get our eyes off people and on the Lord and confess we are a sinner (Rom. 3:23).

Secondly, Isaiah had a live coal from the altar placed on his lips by one of the seraphim that cleansed him. Today we are cleansed by the blood of Jesus (1 John 1:7). Jesus is the only way to have an encounter with God (John 14:6). There are not many ways to God, only Jesus. The plan of salvation is as simple as ABC. A-admit you are a sinner, B-Believe on the Lord, and C-confess that Jesus is the resurrected Savior. Our encounter with the risen Savior must not stop with just a one-time encounter, but we must have a relationship with the Lord. This comes through prayer and studying the word of God. Some people have the teaching but do not have the touch of God upon them. Your teaching can be correct but not have God's touch on you. There's no way I can help people without first having an encounter with God. The Apostle Paul didn't help anyone before he first received from the Lord (1 Cor. 15:3).

Be an encourager

Hebrews 3:13 tells us to "...exhort one another daily...". Exhort means to come closely alongside of someone for the purpose of speaking counsel, advice, or comfort. Exhort is sometimes translated encouragement in the New Testament. Jesus used the word comforter in John 14:16 to describe the work of the Holy Spirit which is a derivative of the same word exhort. These verses make it very clear that we should be encouraging others daily. It doesn't take much to encourage someone. Sometimes just a phone call, email, short note, or taking someone to lunch can encourage someone. Our problem is that we get so focused on our own needs we forget about the needs of others. It's easy to say you love someone. Love is not just words but done in deeds (1 John 3:18).

In other words, love is a demonstration not a declaration. Jesus taught about helping one another. He said to feed the hungry, give the thirsty a drink, take in the stranger, clothe the naked, and visit the sick and prisoner (Matt. 25:35-45). The key is not just to encourage once a week or once a month but daily. Purpose your heart to encourage people every day. Make it a way of living. Be a daily encourager, and you will be pleasantly surprised by how many people you will help.

Fred Rogers was the creator and host of the preschool television series Mister Rogers' Neighborhood, which ran from 1968 to 2001. When he received his Lifetime Achievement Emmy for his television series, one of the first things he said was, "So many people have helped me to come to this night. Some of you are here, some are far away, some are even in heaven. All of us have special ones who loved us into being. Would you just take along with me, 10 seconds, to think of the people who have helped you become who you are? Those who have cared about you and wanted what was best for you in life. 10 seconds of silence. I'll watch the time. Whomever you've been thinking about, how pleased they must be to know the difference you feel they have made."

Obviously, over the years, millions of children were helped and inspired by the tender voice of a man who reached out to encourage them. Fred Rogers acknowledged on national television that he could not have reached his audience of children without the help of others.

Be a Light in a Dark World

Jesus said His followers are the light of the world. A light which shines so bright that people would see our good works, which would in turn glorify our Heavenly Father (Matt. 5:14-16). We may never know this side of heaven who we brought to Christ by being a light. Tim Tebow is a professional baseball player as well as a former quarterback for the Denver Broncos, New York Jets, and the University of Florida. He is an avid Christian and a light in the world. During the 2008 college football season, he painted Phil. 4:13 under each eye. For the College Football National Championship on January 8, 2009 he changed the verse to John 3:16.

During the national championship game, 94 million people googled John 3:16. He was a light in the world. Exactly three years later on January 8, 2012, Tebow led the Denver Broncos to its first AFC West title. After the victory, Tim was making his way to an interview when he was stopped and told some startling statistics about the game. This person shared with Tebow that he had thrown the football for a total of 316 passing yards, he averaged 3.16 rushing yards, he had a 31.6 yards per completion, the time of possession was 31:06, the tv ratings were 31.6 and 90 million people googled John 3:16. God is looking for someone to help by being a light in a dark world. God is looking for helpers.

Be a Servant

Jesus didn't come to earth 2000 years ago to be served, but to serve (Mark 10:45). He came not to do His will, but his Father's (Matthew 26:39). Jesus came to seek and save that which was lost

(Luke 19:10). Through His serving, Jesus constantly helped people. Jesus said the greatest among us would be the person who serves (Matthew 23:11). I have found that when I help other people by serving them, God blesses me and I am helped as well (Luke 6:38). For instance, when I teach someone about God's grace, I receive a deeper understanding about grace. When I help someone, who is having marital problems, my own marriage is strengthened. The next time you are feeling unloved or spiritually or mentally fatigued, go help someone by serving them. God has given the gift of helpers to serve others (1 Cor. 12:28).

Someone or maybe even numerous people have helped you in your troubling times. As we have read in previous chapters, God has numerous ways of helping people. Will you be one of His God Helpers?

Remember, help is always closer than you think.

Discussion questions:

1. What happens when we are a light in the world?

2. Why did Jesus come into the world?

3. Who did Jesus say would be the greatest person among us?

4. What are some of the ways I could help people?

5. Has God given to some of the people of the church, the gift of helpers?

God Helpers

ABOUT THE AUTHOR

E.C. Russell has four decades of ministerial experience which includes pastoral ministry in five churches; missions work in Cuba, Honduras, and the Canary Islands; service as a police chaplain with three different law enforcement agencies; and more than 15 years of radio ministry. He has a Bachelor of Arts in Pastoral Ministry and a Master of Arts in Ministry.

Today, millions of people are struggling and searching for help. This book is about different methods God uses to help hurting people from all walks of life who are experiencing heartaches and facing day-to-day struggles. In this book, he shares personal tragedies in his life and the lives of others that were changed through God's various helpers. Revelations of God's help will unfold as you read through each chapter.

Remember, help is always closer than you think.

Pastor Russell would love to hear from you!

Please feel free to reach out to him and let him know what this book has meant to you.

ecrussell@bellsouth.net

~Follow Pastor Russell on Facebook~

EC Russell